cat naps...

PUBLISHED BY
Wise Publications
8/9 Frith Street, London W1D 3JB, England.

EXCLUSIVE DISTRIBUTORS
Music Sales Limited
Distribution Centre, Newmarket Road,
Bury St. Edmunds, Suffolk IP33 3YB, England.
Music Sales Pty Limited
120 Rothschild Avenue, Rosebery,
NSW 2018, Australia.

Order No. MFA10003
ISBN 1-84609-145-4
This book © Copyright 2005 Wise Publications,
a division of Music Sales Limited.

DESIGNED AND PACKAGED BY
Balley Design Associates
CREATIVE DIRECTOR **Simon Balley**
DESIGNER **Karen Hood**
PROJECT EDITOR **Hilary Mandleberg**

All animal images copyright
Digital Vision and Getty Images

Book printed in China.

CD CREDITS
Executive producer: Akira Komatsu
Composition: Hiroki Sakaguchi
Performance: Hiroki Sakaguchi (Keyboard), Chikara Suda
(Cello & Gutstring), Shigeru Oikawa (Recorder/Traverso),
Tohru Sakurada (Lute), Hiroshi Fukuzawa (viola da gamba),
Takeshi Ishikawa (percussion)
Engineer: Teruaki Igarashi (bazooka Studio & Paradise
Studio 2003 Spring)
Co-operation: Azabu Veterinary University Man & Animal
Relationship Research Team (+ Sakura, Layna and Kuro)
Total planning: Satoshi Yoshida (Shinko Music)
Notes: Some of the tracks in this CD contain sounds that are
only audible to animals

cat naps...

Wise Publications
part of The Music Sales Group
London / New York / Paris / Sydney / Copenhagen / Berlin / Madrid / Tokyo

Cats are just little hair factories.

In the middle of a world that has always been a bit mad, the cat walks with confidence.

Cats are a **mysterious** kind of folk. There is more passing in their minds than we are aware of. It comes no doubt from their being so familiar with warlocks and **witches**.

Two cats can **live** as cheaply as one, and their owner has twice as **much fun.**

To **bathe** a cat takes brute force, perseverance, courage of conviction and a cat.

The last ingredient is usually hardest to come by.

A dog is a man's best friend.

A cat is a **cat's** best friend.

Watch a cat when it enters a room for the first time. It searches and smells about, it is not quiet for a moment, it trusts nothing until it has examined and made acquaintance with everything.

17

Cats seem to go on the principle
that it never does any harm
to ask for what you want.

People that <u>hate</u> cats will come
back as mice in their next <u>life</u>.

You will **always** be lucky
if you know how to make
friends with strange cats.

Cats are intended to
teach us that not everything
in nature has a function.

Cats always seem so very wise,
when staring with their half-closed
eyes. Can they be thinking ...

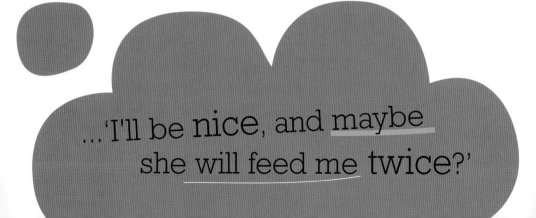

... 'I'll be nice, and maybe
she will feed me twice?'

A cat is more intelligent than people believe, and can be taught any crime.

Even a cat

is a lion

in her own lair.

A cat is there when you call her - if she doesn't have something better to do.

Cats are possessed of a shy, retiring nature, cajoling, haughty, and capricious, difficult to fathom. They reveal themselves only to certain favoured individuals, and are repelled by the faintest suggestion of insult or even by the most trifling deception.

There is no **snooze** button
on a cat who wants breakfast.

Solitude is often the best society.

A kitten is chiefly
remarkable for rushing
about like mad at nothing
whatsoever, and generally

stopping before it gets there.

To a dog, you're one of the family.

To a cat, you're one of the help.

Dogs come when they're called –

cats take a message and get back to you later.

As every cat owner knows,
nobody **owns** a cat.

Cats are connoisseurs of comfort.

Cats are like Baptists.
You KNOW they raise hell,
but you can never catch
them at it.

Dogs have Owners,
Cats have Staff.

53

If cats could talk,

they wouldn't.

Want a mental
challenge?
Try herding cats!

The cat has too much spirit to have no heart.

I've met many thinkers
and many cats,
but the **wisdom of cats**
is infinitely superior.

No matter how much cats fight, there always seem to be plenty of kittens.

A cat's a cat and that's that.

Cats know not
how to pardon.

No one can have experienced
to the fullest the true sense
of achievement and satisfaction
who have never pursued and
successfully caught his tail.

In a cat's eye,

all things belong to cats.

A cat pours his body on the floor like <u>water</u>. It is restful just to see him.

Solitude is

independence.

Cats are irresponsible and recognize no authority, yet are completely dependent on others for their material needs. Cats cannot be made to do anything useful. Cats are mean for the fun of it.

Cats aren't clean,

they're just covered

with cat spit.

I believe cats to be spirits come to earth.

A cat, I am sure, could walk on a cloud without coming through.

To cats,

people are just furniture

that does tricks.

A kitten is a rosebud in the garden of the animal kingdom.

The cat could very well be man's best friend but would never stoop to...

...admitting it.

Cats are rather delicate creatures and they are subject to a good many ailments, but I never heard of one who suffered from insomnia.

Thousands of years ago,
cats were worshipped as gods.
Cats have **never** forgotten this.

A computer and a cat are somewhat alike — they both purr, and like to be stroked, and spend a lot of the day motionless. They also have secrets they don't necessarily share.

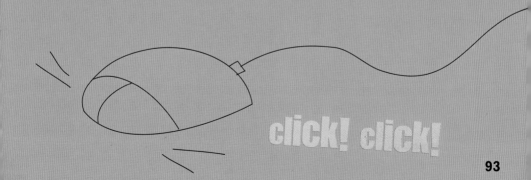

click! click!

There are people who reshape
the world by force or argument,

but the cat just lies there, dozing,

and the world quietly
reshapes itself to suit his
comfort and convenience.

who said what?

p.4 James Davis; p.7 Roseanne Anderson; p.9 Sir Walter Scott; p.11 Lloyd Alexander; p.13 Stephen Baker; p.15 Robert J. Vogel; p.17 Jean Jacques Rousseau; p.19 Joseph Wood Krutch; p.21 Faith Resnick; p.23 Colonial American proverb; p.24 Garrison Keillor; p.27 Bette Midler; p.29 Mark Twain; p.30 Indian proverb; p.33 Bill Adler; p.35 Pierre Loti; p.37 Anonymous; p.39 Anonymous; p.41 Agnes Repplier; p.43 Anonymous; p.45 Mary Bly; p.47 Ellen Perry Berkeley; p.49 James Herriot; p.50 James Patterson; p.53 Anonymous; p.55 Nan Porter; p.57 Anonymous; p.59 Ernest Menaul; p.61 Hippolyte Taine; p.63 Abraham Lincoln; p.65 American folk saying; p.67 Jean de la Fontaine; p.69 Rosalind Welcher; p.71 English proverb; p.72 William Lyon Phelps; p.74 Herman Hesse; p.77 P. J. O'Rourke; p.79 John S. Nichols; p.81 Jules Verne; p.83 Anonymous; p.85 Robert Southey; p.87 Doug Larson; p.89 Joseph Wood Krutch; p.91 Anonymous; p.93 John Updike; p.94 Allen and Ivy Dodd

Every effort has been made to contact or trace all copyright holders. In future editions the publishers will be glad to make good any errors or omissions that are brought to their attention.

CD track listing

1 / "GORO GORO" Fantasy **2 /** Sleeping On The Roof
3 / Dream Catcher **4 /** Cat's Cradle

All tracks: (Hiroki Sakaguchi) Shinko Music Publishing Co., Ltd.

Also available: dog daze... MFA10002 ISBN 1-84609-144-6